NIGHT OF THE KACHINA

NICHOLE SALAS

≋PACESETTERS

CHILDRENS PRESS, CHICAGO

Childrens Press Edition

Series Director: Tom Belina
Designer: Richard Kharibian
Cover and illustrations: David Cunningham

ISBN 0–516–5261

Printed in the United States of America.

1. 9 8 7 6 5 4 3 2 1

CONTENTS

CHAPTER **1**

TO THE LAND OF ANCESTORS

"But why do you want to go?" Lenny Carlson asked his friend, Ray Brant.

Ray thought about Lenny's question. It was a good question. Why *did* he want to go to talk to his great-grandfather? He had never met the man. He had never even seen him—not once in his whole life. He had only heard about him from his mother and father. And his father's father had also talked about him a lot. They said that he knew all about the Old Ways.

"Ray!" Lenny said. "Are your ears blocked up? Can't you hear me, man?"

"I can hear you," Ray said.

"So answer my question, OK? I want to know why you want to go to New Mexico. I mean, to see a man you don't even know."

"He is my great-grandfather," Ray said. "I already told you that."

"I know. I know you did. But I still don't get it. I mean I really do not get it at all."

"I'm not sure I do either," Ray said. When he spoke, his voice was soft. "But I think—" he began and then he stopped.

"You think what?" Lenny asked him.

"I think it has something to do with finding out who I am," Ray said.

Lenny laughed and slapped his leg. "You don't have to go all the way to New Mexico to find out who you are. I can tell you who you are. You're Ray Brant."

"Cut it out," Ray said, his voice still soft. "You know what I mean. I want to know something about my past. Something about the history of my people. My great-grandfather can tell me."

Lenny stopped laughing. He said, "You mean about what it's like to be an American Indian."

"Sort of," Ray said. "I mean I guess so. But that's only a part of it. I guess I want to know about my ancestors. I've made up my mind. I'm going to New Mexico. I'm going to talk to my great-grandfather."

"What's his name?" Lenny asked.

"Black Bear," Ray answered.

"That's all? Just Black Bear?"

"Just Black Bear. I think it's a good name."

"The more I think about it, the more I think you're right. I like it. Black Bear. A good name."

"Do you want to go to New Mexico with me?" Ray said.

"I thought you would never ask," Lenny answered. He stood up. "When do we go?"

Ray also stood up. "Why not right now?"

"Sounds good to me," Lenny answered. "How long will we be gone?"

"No more than a week or ten days. Probably less than that."

"See you later, man," Lenny said. "I've got to pack some clothes and things."

"Me too," Ray said. "Meet me back here in an hour."

When Lenny had gone, Ray began to pack his clothes. When he had packed everything, he waited for Lenny to return.

When Lenny did return, they got in Ray's car and drove away. Soon they were miles from home heading for New Mexico.

"How long will it take us to get there?" Lenny asked.

"Almost two days," Ray said. "We can take turns driving."

"I'm hungry," Lenny said.

"Already? You have got to be out of your mind! You just ate an hour ago."

"If I don't get something to eat pretty soon, I might pass out." Lenny smiled.

"OK," Ray said with a laugh. "There is a place up ahead where you can eat."

Ray drove to the place. They went inside. When they had finished their food, they got back in the car.

When Ray got tired, Lenny drove. Later, they traded places again.

They drove for the whole day. They only stopped once to eat dinner. That night they went to sleep in the car. During the next afternoon, they came to the town in New Mexico where Black Bear lived.

They drove to Black Bear's house. Ray went up to the front door and knocked. No answer. He knocked again. Still no answer.

"Maybe we came all this way for nothing," Lenny said. "He's not home. And I'm hungry again. So let's—"

Just then a woman came out of the house next door.

Ray went over to speak to her.

"Do you know the man who lives in that house over there?" he asked the woman. "His name is Black Bear."

"Yes, I know him," the woman said.

"Do you know where he is?" Ray asked. "He is my great-grandfather. I've come a long way to visit him."

"I'm sorry," the woman said, shaking her head. "You're too late."

"What do you mean?"

"Black Bear is very sick," the woman told Ray. "The doctor wanted him to go to the hospital. But Black Bear wouldn't go. He wouldn't even take the pills the doctor gave him. He doesn't believe in pills."

"But where is he?" Ray asked.

"Black Bear told me he thought he was going to die," the woman said. "But he said he didn't want to die here. He wanted to die where his ancestors once lived. So he went there."

"To die?" Ray asked, not able to believe what he had heard.

"Yes," the woman said. "He went to the old Indian ruins in the desert. They are the ruins of Pueblo Bonita. They are in Chaco Canyon."

"Can you tell me how to get to Chaco Canyon?" Ray asked.

The woman told him how to get to the ruins. "Chaco Canyon," she said, "is not far from here. Just a few miles."

"Thank you," Ray said to her. He went back to Lenny and said, "Come on, we have to go to Chaco Canyon. We have to try to save Black Bear's life."

Then Ray told Lenny what the woman had said about Black Bear.

"OK," Lenny said. "I guess I'm not really as hungry as I thought I was. Let's go!"

They got in the car. A minute later, the car screamed down the road toward Chaco Canyon. But would they be in time?

CHAPTER **2**

BLACK BEAR

Black Bear sat very still inside the ruins of Pueblo Bonita.

Broken rock walls were behind him. In the walls were small open spaces. The spaces were windows.

Black Bear looked up at the broken walls. He looked at the windows. He could almost see faces at the windows. He thought he could hear voices calling to him from inside Pueblo Bonita. Voices of the Old Ones.

"I am here," he said out loud. "I have come home to my ancestors."

There was no other sound but that of his voice. Nothing.

Black Bear said no more. The sound of his voice made him feel sad. He felt sad because there was no one in the ruins to speak to him.

But he knew he had done a good thing. It was a good thing to come back to the land of his ancestors.

They are all gone now, he thought. And soon, I too will be gone.

He no longer felt sad. He was almost happy. Because he knew he had done a good thing. He had come to die in the house of his people.

He sat down and looked around him.

Far away was one of the high walls of Chaco Canyon. Behind him were the ruins. Behind the ruins was the other wall of Chaco Canyon. Under his feet was the sand of the desert. A few small plants grew here and there.

The sun felt hot on his body. But the sun was about to go down. Already there were dark places in the ruins. Night was only hours away. When night came, the desert would grow cold.

And dark.

Black Bear did not want to think about the night or the dark.

He took a knife from his pocket. He began to carve the piece of wood he held in his hand.

He carved the wood for more than an hour. Then he took some beads from his pocket. He put the beads on the kachina doll he had made. He also put some feathers on it.

Then he took some little cans of paint from his pocket. He painted the face of the kachina doll blue and red.

He spoke to it. He said some old secret words to it. He asked the kachina to take care of him.

Suddenly, behind him, there was a noise. He looked around. As he did so, a rock fell from one of the broken walls.

But there is no one here but me, he thought. Why did that rock fall down? Perhaps, he thought, a desert animal made it fall.

But he began to feel a little bit afraid. Of what am I afraid, he asked himself. The night that will come? A rock that fell down? Or something worse?

He didn't know for sure.

He looked again at the kachina doll he held in his hand. He whispered some more secret words to it. He asked the kachina to keep him safe.

Suddenly, another rock fell down behind him with a crash.

Black Bear got to his feet.

He walked to where the two rocks had hit the ground. He looked up at the high wall above him. He listened.

He could hear nothing.

He climbed up to the top of the wall. Then he climbed down inside one of the rooms of Pueblo Bonita. He looked around. He saw nothing. He heard nothing. He went from room to room.

Once he thought he saw something. But did he really? He wasn't sure.

My old eyes, he thought. My old eyes play tricks on me.

He was about to leave the room when his foot hit something. He looked down. There was a pile of dirt at his feet. He got down on the ground. He began to dig in the dirt.

Soon he found a pot. He took it out of the dirt. It was a white pot. On it one of his ancestors had long ago painted beautiful black marks.

Black Bear wished that he could make pots the way his ancestors once did. People liked the pots even now. He knew that sometimes people came to Pueblo Bonita just to find these pots. If they found any, they took them away with them. But that was against the law. It was also against the Old Ways.

He climbed out of the ruins. He took the pot with him. He would keep it beside him. The pot and the kachina doll would keep him company tonight. They would remind him of his ancestors who lived long ago.

He was about to put the pot down on the ground. Something fell out of it.

To his surprise, Black Bear saw that paper money was on the ground. It had come from the pot. There was a lot of money. Black Bear counted it. There were thousands of dollars. He put all the money back in the pot.

He thought for a minute. Then, with the pot in his hand, he went back into the ruins. He went to the place where he had found the pot. He got down on the ground. He began to dig. He found five more black and white pots.

In each of them he found thousands of dollars. At first, he didn't know what to do.

But finally he put all the pots back in the ground. He covered them up with dirt. The pots, he decided, were none of his business. He would leave them where they were.

He was about to leave the ruins when he heard a sound. It came from outside. Some-one—or something—was out there. Black Bear stood still and listened.

He heard a rock fall. Then another one fell.

Who was out there? *What* was out there?

He didn't know. But he would find out. He climbed out of the ruins. He could see no one.

Then he heard the sound again. At the same time, a hand grabbed his arm.

CHAPTER **3**

TROUBLE IN THE RUINS

Black Bear turned around fast. "Who are you?" he asked.

"My name is Ray Brant," Ray said. "Are you Black Bear?"

"Yes, I'm Black Bear. But I don't know you."

"I'm your great-grandson," Ray said. "And this is my friend, Lenny Carlson. We were looking for you."

"Hello," Lenny said. "I'm glad to meet you, Black Bear."

"My great-grandson," Black Bear said, looking at Ray. "I'm very glad to meet you at last."

"We went to your house," Ray told Black Bear. "A woman told us you had come out here to Chaco Canyon."

"Did she tell you why I came to this place?" Black Bear asked.

"Yes," Lenny said. "She said you came out here to—" He didn't finish his sentence.

Black Bear smiled at him. "I am an old man. It is time for me to go. I have been very sick."

"I wanted to talk to you about that," Ray said. "You should see your doctor."

"I did," Black Bear said. "He gave me some pills to take."

"Didn't the pills help you?" Ray asked.

"Not enough," Black Bear answered. He looked up at the sky. The sun was almost gone from it. "Maybe," he said, "the kachina will help me live."

"The kachina?" Lenny said to Black Bear. "What is a kachina?"

Black Bear showed Lenny and Ray the kachina doll he had carved. "I made the doll to look like one of the kachinas," he told them. "The kachinas are Indian spirits. This kachina has always taken good care of my people."

"I have heard of kachina dances," Ray said.

"Have you ever seen one?" Black Bear asked.

Ray shook his head.

"Men play the parts of the spirits in the dances," Black Bear said. "They put on masks and costumes. Then they look just like the kachinas. They dance. They ask the kachinas to help our people."

"It's getting dark," Lenny said. "Not only that, I'm getting—"

"Don't tell me," Ray said. "I know. You're getting hungry again."

"Right!" Lenny said. "How did you guess?"

Ray laughed. So did Lenny.

Then Ray said to Black Bear, "Let's go back to your house now. Then we can—"

Black Bear shook his head.

"But—" Ray began.

"No," Black Bear said. "I will stay here until—" He said no more.

Ray looked at Lenny. Lenny said nothing. Ray turned back to Black Bear.

"If you don't go with us," he said, "then we will stay here with you."

Lenny looked at Ray. His eyes got wide. "Stay here? You don't mean it. Tell me you don't mean it, man. It's spooky here. I don't think we should—"

"You should not stay here tonight," Black Bear said. His voice was low. "At night, it is cold here. And there may be trouble."

"Trouble?" Ray said.

"What kind of trouble?" Lenny asked, looking around him.

"I have found something," Black Bear said. "It may be the cause of much trouble."

"What did you find?" Ray asked.

"Come with me. I will show you both." Black Bear got up. He began to climb into the old stone ruins.

"Be careful," Ray called out to him.

"I will be careful," Black Bear said. "Come with me."

Ray and Lenny followed Black Bear into the old stone ruins.

When Black Bear had led them to where the money was, he began to dig in the ground.

He found a pot. He took the money from it.

"I don't believe it!" Lenny yelled. "You're rich, Black Bear!"

"No, I'm not. This money is not mine."

"Then who does it belong to?" Ray asked.

"I don't know," Black Bear answered.

"How did it get here?" Lenny asked.

Black Bear said he didn't know how the money got into the ruins. "I found it here just before you two came," he said. "I think it could be the cause of trouble."

"Then let's get out of here while we still can," Lenny said.

"He is right, Black Bear," Ray said. "We really should get out of here. Let me take you back home."

"You go," Black Bear said. "You and your friend. I will stay here."

Ray was about to say something when they all heard a sound.

"It came from up there," Ray said. He pointed to the top of the wall.

"Look out!" Lenny yelled. "That wall is about to fall on us!"

The three of them began to run. As they ran, the wall fell down upon them.

CHAPTER **4**

THE HOUSE OF THE DEAD

They got out of the way just in time.

Big stones crashed down behind them. The noise the stones made as they fell was very loud.

They ran fast to escape the stones.

A small one hit Black Bear on the leg. He almost fell, but Ray caught him.

They climbed up a wall that looked strong. From it, they jumped to the ground.

"We made it!" Lenny yelled. "We got out of there alive!"

"That sure was a close call," Ray said.

"Those walls are very old," Black Bear said. "I guess that's why the wall fell on us."

"I know the walls are old," Ray said, "but—"

"What is the matter, Ray?" Black Bear asked. "What is it?"

Ray was looking up at the broken wall. "Just before that wall fell," he said, "I thought I heard something."

"Like what?" Lenny asked him.

"Like someone moving around up there."

"I didn't hear anything," Black Bear said.

"Listen to me a minute," Lenny said. "We got out of the ruins all safe and sound. Now let's get out of Chaco Canyon the same way before—"

"Not yet," Ray said. "I want to find out something."

"What is it?" Black Bear asked him.

But Ray didn't answer. Instead, he began to climb back into the ruins. A minute later, he called back to Black Bear and Lenny.

They joined him in the ruins.

"Look at that," he said to them. He pointed to a spot in the ruins. "We were down there when this wall fell on us."

"So what?" said Lenny.

"Look at these footprints up here," Ray said. "There in the sand. They are not ours."

Black Bear thought for a minute. "Maybe," he said, "that wall did not fall down all by itself."

"I don't think it did," Ray said. "Someone was up here and pushed it down on us."

"The person who did it," Lenny said, "had boots on. You can tell from those footprints."

Black Bear said, "Let's look around. Maybe we can find the person who wanted to kill us."

"I don't want to find anyone," Lenny said. "I just want to get out of here. It's dark already."

"Take it easy, Lenny," Ray said. He began to walk through the ruins. Black Bear went the other way. Lenny left the ruins.

Ten minutes later, Ray came out of the ruins. So did Black Bear.

"I didn't find anyone," Black Bear said.

"I didn't either," Ray said.

"Good!" Lenny said. "Let's hope no one finds *us* under an old wall again."

Ray stood still without saying anything. He looked at the ruins. "Pueblo Bonita must have been beautiful once," he said.

"Yes, it must have been," Black Bear said. "When people lived here." His voice sounded sad. "Did you know that Pueblo Bonita means 'beautiful town' in Spanish?"

"No, I didn't know that," Ray said. "What were the people like who lived here?"

"They grew all their own food," Black Bear said. "They did not make war. They were fine artists. You saw the pots they made. They also made baskets and other beautiful things."

"What happened to the people?" Ray asked.

"No one knows for sure," Black Bear said. "They just went away from here."

"When?" Ray asked. "Why?"

"They went away hundreds of years ago," Black Bear answered. "Some people think that the land got too dry. They think the Indians left to find better places for their gardens."

"Pueblo Bonita must have been like a great big apartment house," Ray said.

"It was," Black Bear said. "It had eight hundred rooms. Hundreds of people lived in the rooms. Now—now it is the house of the dead."

"Please don't talk like that," Lenny said. "That's spooky talk." He looked at the ruins. "Look!" he yelled. "I just saw a light in there— way in the back."

"Are you sure?" Black Bear asked him.

Lenny said he was sure.

They all watched the ruins for several minutes, looking into the growing dark.

"Look!" Lenny said. "There it is again. The light I saw!"

This time Ray and Black Bear also saw the light in the ruins.

"Someone is in there," Ray said. "Let's go in and find out who it is."

"Now wait a minute, Ray," Lenny said. "Don't you think we should—?"

But Ray had already started into the ruins.

"Wait!" Black Bear yelled.

Ray stopped and came back. "What is it?"

"It might be a kachina in there," Black Bear whispered. "Maybe it has come back here to the place of our ancestors."

"I said before that this place was spooky," Lenny said in a low voice. "Now I say it is even more spooky in the dark."

"There are bad kachinas as well as good ones," Black Bear said. "Some of the kachinas hurt the Indians. Maybe it was a bad one who made the wall fall down on us."

"I don't think so," Ray said. "No, it wasn't a kachina."

"But how do you know for sure that it wasn't?" Black Bear asked.

"Kachinas—do they wear boots?"

Black Bear said, "You're right, Ray. I forgot about those footprints we saw."

"It's getting cold," Lenny said. "Maybe we could come back here tomorrow. Or next *year* might be even better."

"You're not afraid, are you?" Ray asked Lenny.

"Me? Afraid? No, not me. I'm not afraid. Me, I'm scared stiff is what I am."

"You two wait here," Ray said. "I'm going in there to have a look around."

Ray ran to where he had parked his car. He got a flashlight from the car.

He returned to the ruins and went inside them. His flashlight made the ruins almost as bright as day.

He came to the place where Black Bear had found the pots full of money. All of them were gone!

He ran from the ruins. He told Black Bear and Lenny about the pots.

"I wonder what happened to them," Black Bear said.

"Forget about those pots and the money," Lenny said. "Let's get out of here before something happens to *us!*"

CHAPTER 5

A TIME TO DIE

Lenny started to walk to the car. He looked back. "Are you coming?" he asked Ray.

"Something is wrong with Black Bear," Ray said. "I think he is sick."

Black Bear said, "I feel strange. My head feels funny. Let me sit down here for a minute."

Black Bear sat down on the ground. Ray sat down beside him.

Lenny came back. "He looks very bad," he whispered to Ray. "We should take him to a doctor."

Black Bear heard what Lenny had whispered. "No," he said. "What must be, must be. My time has come."

"What about his pills?" Lenny said. "They might help him."

"Good idea," Ray answered. He turned to Black Bear. "Do you have your pills with you?"

"No, I don't," said Black Bear. "They are back at my house."

"Come on then," Ray said. "We will drive you home. Then you can take your pills."

"No, it is too late for pills," Black Bear said. "Already my legs feel weak. I don't think I can walk. It is time to die."

"We can't just let you die," Ray said.

Lenny said, "Maybe we could—"

Black Bear said, "Lenny, will you bring me my kachina doll? It's over there beside the ruins."

Lenny looked over at the ruins. They looked very strange in the white light of the moon. "OK," he said at last. "I'll go and get it."

"I'll drive to your house," Ray told Black Bear. "I'll get your pills and bring them back here to you. Lenny can stay here with you while I'm gone."

"No," Black Bear said. "You can see that Lenny is afraid to stay. So take him with you."

"But—"

"Do as I say," Black Bear said. "Don't worry about me. The kachina will watch over me."

Just then Lenny returned. In his hand was the kachina doll. He gave it to Black Bear.

"Go now, both of you," Black Bear said.

Ray got Black Bear to tell him where the pills were in his house. He also gave Lenny the key to his house. He really didn't think the pills would do any good. But he knew Ray wanted to help him so he let him try.

As Ray and Lenny drove away, Black Bear whispered the old secret words to the kachina doll. He thought that the kachina smiled up at him. It felt very warm in his hands.

Ray drove very fast. Soon they reached Black Bear's house.

They got out of the car and ran to the front door.

Lenny opened the door with the key that Black Bear had given him.

They went inside. Lenny went into Black Bear's bedroom to get the pills.

When he had gone, Ray looked at the pictures on the walls. There were a lot of them. In one, a young Indian sat on a white horse.

Ray suddenly knew who the man on the horse was. It was Black Bear when he was young.

Beside the picture on the wall hung a costume. It had many feathers on it. The feathers were black and white. It also had many beads on it. The beads were red and black.

Next to the costume was a mask. It was painted blue and red and white. It had holes for eyes.

Just then Lenny came out of the bedroom. "I've got the pills," he said.

"Look at that," Ray said to him. He pointed to the mask and the costume. "I think I've seen that mask and costume somewhere before."

"Me too," Lenny said. "But where?"

"I've got it!" Ray said. "The mask and the costume are just like the kachina doll that Black Bear carved."

"Look over there at that picture on the wall," Lenny said.

Ray looked at it. In the picture, Black Bear was wearing the costume of the kachina. It was the same costume that now hung on the wall. In his hands, he held the mask.

"He must have been a kachina dancer when he was young," Ray said.

A minute later, they left the house. They drove back to Chaco Canyon.

When they got there, they found Black Bear on the ground.

"Is he OK?" Lenny whispered to Ray.

Just then Black Bear opened his eyes.

"Here, take your pills," Ray said. "They will help you."

"I don't need any pills," Black Bear said. "I'm feeling better."

"Please take them," Ray said. "The doctor told you that you should."

"All right, Ray," Black Bear said. "I'll take them if it makes you feel better." He smiled and took two of the pills.

A few minutes later, he said, "I think I can walk now. Will you help me up, Ray?"

Ray helped Black Bear get to his feet. Then the three of them started toward the car.

But before they reached it, a shot rang out.

"There is a man up there on the top of the canyon wall!" Lenny yelled. "He has a gun!"

"Let's try to get to the car," Ray said. "We can hide behind it."

Another shot rang out.

A bullet kicked up dirt at their feet.

"Are you OK, Black Bear?" Ray asked as they ran.

Black Bear said that he was OK.

"Lenny?" Ray said. "Are you OK? Lenny?"

Ray looked back. He saw Lenny running away from them.

Ray and Black Bear got to the car. They ran around behind it.

"Where is Lenny?" Black Bear asked.

"I guess he was so scared he didn't know what he was doing," Ray answered. "He ran away."

"Can you see him?" Black Bear asked.

"No," Ray said, "I can't. All I can see is that man up there on top of the canyon wall. The man with the gun."

CHAPTER **6**

SURPRISE FROM THE SKY

"Let's get out of here," Ray said to Black Bear. "Let's run for it."

"I think that's what the man with the gun wants," Black Bear said. "I think he is trying to scare us out of here. Like he did to your friend."

"Well, what are we waiting for?" Ray said. Another bullet hit the rocks close to them.

"Follow me," Black Bear said. They both made a run for some rocks. They got down behind them. Another shot rang out. They got back up and headed away from the ruins.

But then Black Bear stopped. "Wait," he said to Ray. "We have gone far enough. The man with the gun thinks he has scared us off. Let's double back and find out what is going on."

They were soon back near the ruins of Pueblo Bonita. But when they looked up at the canyon wall, the man was gone.

Five minutes later, they heard the car start.
"He is taking my car," Ray said to Black
Bear. "What shall we do?"

"Nothing," said Black Bear. "Let him take it.
You don't want to get shot. Let's look for your
friend Lenny."

As they looked, they heard a sound.

"That sounds like an airplane," Black Bear
said. "It's coming this way."

They looked up at the sky. A small airplane
flew past the moon. It came close to the ground.
It landed in the canyon near Pueblo Bonita.

"We had better get out of sight," Ray said.

They got down behind the pile of rocks again.
They watched the pilot get out of the airplane.
The pilot, they saw, was a woman. Then a man
came out of the ruins. He walked toward the
airplane. In the man's hand was a gun.

"That's the man who shot at us," Ray whispered. "He's back."

"Look," Black Bear said. "He has boots on.
He must be the one who made the wall fall
down on us before. Those were his footprints we
saw behind the wall."

"You're right," Ray said. "He must have
been in the ruins—watching us all the time."

"Keep your voice down," Black Bear said. "He thinks he scared us off. He doesn't know that we are still here."

"What are those two doing?" Ray asked.

The man put his gun inside the airplane. Then he and the woman walked into the ruins. They were lost to sight.

But a few minutes later, they both came out of the ruins. In their hands were some of the black and white pots.

"Those are the pots with the money in them," Ray said.

The man and the woman put the pots in the airplane. Then they went back into the ruins again for the rest of the pots.

Black Bear got to his feet. "I'm going to try to get that gun," he said.

"Don't! They could kill you!"

But Black Bear was already gone.

Ray ran after him. They met at the airplane. Black Bear took the gun out of the airplane.

"Stay down behind the airplane," Black Bear told Ray.

When the man and woman came back to the airplane, Black Bear was ready for them. "Don't move," he said.

The man and woman both stopped. They were too surprised to say anything.

Ray came to stand beside Black Bear.

"See if they have any other guns on them," Black Bear said.

Ray walked over to the man and woman. He found that they had no other guns. He told Black Bear.

"Who are you?" Black Bear asked the man.

"My name is Mac Beghay," the man said.

"You're an Indian like me and Ray," Black Bear said.

"No, not like you two, old man," Mac said. He laughed at Black Bear. "Not like you at all. I'm a *smart* Indian."

Black Bear looked at the woman who stood beside Mac.

"She is a good friend of mine," Mac said. "Her name is Liz. She helped me rob the Pueblo Tribal Bank. In fact, she planned the whole thing."

"So that's where the money we found came from," Ray said.

"The pots came from the bank, too," Liz said. "They were part of a show of old Indian work at the bank. We plan to sell them for a lot of money."

"After we robbed the bank," Mac said, "Liz drove me out here to hide out. I waited here for her to fly in and take me and the money and the pots out. The police will never find us. We are going to fly out of the state."

"You were the one who made the wall fall on us before, right?" said Ray.

"I wish those rocks had killed you," Mac said. "I would have killed that old man before but I didn't know he was here. I thought you all had gone away in the car."

"I'm glad I'm not an Indian like you," Black Bear said to Mac. "I'm *very* glad I'm not." Then he said to Ray, "Look inside the airplane. See if you can find some rope."

Ray climbed into the airplane. He did find some rope. As he climbed back out, he slipped. He knocked Black Bear down.

Mac grabbed the gun from Black Bear's hand. He pointed it at Ray and Black Bear. "Now it's my turn," he said. "Where do you two want the bullets? In your heads or your hearts?"

"Kill them," Liz said. "Don't waste time talking about it. *Do it!*"

Suddenly an angry scream sounded in the air.

"Look at that!" Liz said. "What is it?"

Something was behind them. It was covered with beads and feathers. Its face was blue and red. Its eyes were black holes.

It screamed again.

So did Liz. And then she began to run away.

CHAPTER 7

THE KACHINA

"It is the kachina!" Black Bear yelled.

"Don't make a move!" Mac said. His eyes were wide and afraid. But he still held the gun.

Liz had started to run away. But she did not get far. Suddenly the kachina was standing in front of her, blocking her way. The kachina waved its arms and let out a scream that was not of this world. Liz stopped in her tracks. She turned back toward the airplane. "Mac! Help me!" she cried. "Don't let that thing get me!"

Mac pointed his gun into the dark night. But he could not see the kachina. He fired a shot in the dark. But the kachina was gone.

Liz came back to the airplane. Her hands were shaking. "It's a spirit," she said to Mac. "It's out to get us because we tried to kill the old man. The kachina protects him."

Mac said, "I don't believe those old stories." But there was a strange look on his face.

Suddenly there was another high scream in the night. Mac fired his gun again. In the flash of light the gun made, he could see the kachina. Its beads of red and black were very bright. So was the paint on its face. Mac fired again. But the kachina was gone again.

Now Mac was really frightened. "Come on, Liz," he said. "Let's get out of here. Get into the airplane. Then I'll take care of these two."

Liz was about to get into the airplane. But just then there was another loud angry scream in the night. This time it was very close.

"Give up," Black Bear said to Mac. "The kachina will not let you escape. You cannot escape from a spirit."

"I'll kill that thing!" Mac said. He fired three times into the night. But the gun fire was wild because Mac's hand was shaking.

Suddenly there was a sound behind him. Mac turned around. There was the kachina coming right at him.

Mac tried to shoot it. But the gun just clicked. It was empty. Mac tried to throw the gun at the kachina. But it was too late. The kachina rushed forward and knocked him to the ground.

Ray jumped on him. "Get me the rope," he yelled to Black Bear. "It's on the ground by the airplane."

Black Bear pushed past Liz. She stood there without moving, her eyes wide. She had been too frightened by the kachina to think about escaping.

In a minute, Mac was tied up. So was Liz. It was all over.

Then Black Bear looked around. "What happened to the kachina?" he said. "I wanted to thank it."

"It's gone," said Ray.

Black Bear and Ray both looked and listened. But the desert was black and still.

But then, far off, they heard something. A half scream, a half cry.

"It's the kachina," said Black Bear. "It is saying good-bye."

CHAPTER 8

MORNING COMES

"One of us has to go for the police," Ray said to Black Bear. "But our car is gone. Mac won't tell us where it is. He says he doesn't know anything about the car."

"He is just saying that to keep us from going to the police," Black Bear said. "If only the kachina would come back. It would make Mac tell us."

"I can tell you where the car is," said a voice from behind them.

"Lenny!" Ray said. "Where have you been? Are you all right?"

Lenny walked forward out of the night, with a smile on his face.

"I'm fine," Lenny said. "I had to run for it when the man with the gun started to fire. I got away from him, but then I got lost. I couldn't find my way back. Then I spotted our car. I followed the dirt road back."

Ray told Lenny what had just happened.

"That is really something!" Lenny said. "Wouldn't you know it? Wouldn't you know that I'd miss out seeing the whole thing . . . ? But come to think of it, I'm not so sure that I'd have wanted to see the kachina. That really sounds spooky."

"The kachina would not have hurt you," Black Bear said. "It is a good spirit. It came only to protect us."

"It still sounds spooky," Lenny said.

"I think we had better leave now," Ray said.

"Like right this very minute," Lenny said.

"Yes, we will go now," Black Bear said. "The long night is over. And I feel better than I ever did in my whole life. Thanks to the kachina."

He looked up at the sky. The stars were gone. So was the moon. In the east, it was almost light. Soon it would be morning.

Ray told Lenny to go and get the car. Then he and Black Bear got the pots and the money.

When Lenny came back with the car, Ray made Liz and Mac get into it. He loaded the gun with some bullets he found in Mac's pocket. Then he got in the back seat with Mac and Liz. Black Bear and Lenny got in the front seat.

Lenny drove away.

"Our first stop will be the police station," Ray said.

When they got to town, Black Bear told Lenny where to find it.

Lenny parked the car. They all got out of it and went into the police station. But Lenny left before Ray and Black Bear finished talking to the police.

When they came outside later, Lenny and the car were gone.

But a minute later, Lenny drove up in the car. He pulled over and parked.

"Where were you?" Ray asked.

"I was hungry," Lenny said. "I went to get something to eat. You didn't need me anyway. I wasn't even there when all this happened, right? So I went for a bite to eat. Come on. Get in. Let's take Black Bear home."

Lenny drove them back to Black Bear's house. When they got there, he gave back the key Black Bear had given him.

"Thank you," Black Bear said as he took the key from Lenny. "Come inside. Lenny, you said you had just had something to eat. But I'll bet you have room for a little more. I'm going to make something for Ray and for me. I'll make a meal for all three of us."

"Sure," said Lenny. "With me, there is always room for more. But I'd like to talk to Ray for a minute first, if it's OK."

Black Bear opened the door to his house. "Fine. I'll get things started." He went inside.

"OK," Ray said to Lenny. "What is it you want to talk about?"

"Kachinas," was Lenny's answer. "I don't want to spoil things for Black Bear."

"What do you mean?"

"That kachina out in the ruins—he was me. I mean I was him."

"*You* were—!"

"When Mac first shot at us, I thought of a plan. I ran away. Then I drove to Black Bear's house."

"But I thought Mac took my car," Ray said.

"No, he didn't. I did. I got Black Bear's kachina mask and costume. Then I drove back to the ruins and put them on."

"You sure scared Liz and Mac out of their minds," Ray said.

"Did I scare you?"

"Not a bit. Well, maybe just a little bit. But Lenny—you could have been killed."

"I took a chance. I felt I had to. Then I put the mask and costume back in the car. I came back to join you and Black Bear."

"Now I can guess where you were when we were at the police station," Ray said.

"I drove back to Black Bear's house. I put the mask and costume back on the wall."

"That was sure a brave thing to do," Ray said. "Man, you are really something *very* special. You really are!"

Lenny's face got red. "Well, I just wanted to tell you what I did. Black Bear believed his kachina would keep him safe. Don't tell him the kachina was me."

"I won't tell him. Not now, for sure—now that he is feeling better again. And you know something? I think you're the one who made Black Bear get better."

"Who me? I'm no doctor," Lenny said. "It was probably those pills he took that made him better."

"I wonder," Ray said.

"Never mind," Lenny said. "Come on. Let's go in the house. Black Bear said he was going to make something for us to eat. And, man, am I ever *hungry!*"

Ray started to say something. "Is that all you ever—?" Then he started laughing. He put his hand on his friend's back. "Lenny," he said, still laughing, "you really are something!"